D0246916

Step-by-Step
Handmade Cards

Tamsin Carter

Heinemann
LIBRARY

www.heinemann.co.uk
Visit our website to find out more information about Heinemann Library books

To order:
Phone 44 (0) 1865 888066

Send a fax to 44 (0) 1865 314091

Visit the Heinemann Bookshop at www.heinemann.co.uk to browse our catalogue and order online

Produced by Search Press Limited in Great Britain 2002.
First published in Great Britain by Heinemann Library, Halley Court, Jordan Hill, Oxford OX2 8EJ, part of Harcourt Education. Heinemann is a registered trademark of Harcourt Education Ltd.

Text copyright © Tamsin Carter 2002
Photographs by Charlotte de la Bédoyère, Search Press Studios
Photographs and design copyright © Search Press Limited 2002

Originated by ClassicScan Ltd, Singapore
Printed in Italy by L.E.G.O.

ISBN 0 43111 180 4
06 05 04 03 02
10 9 8 7 6 5 4 3 2 1

British Library Cataloguing in Publication Data

Carter, Tamsin
Cardmaking. – (Step-by-Step)
1.Greetings cards – Juvenile literature
I.Title
745.5'941

Acknowledgements
The Publishers would like to thank Mary Evans Picture Library for permission to reproduce the photograph on page 5.

Every effort has been made to contact copyright holders of any material reproduced in this book. Any omissions will be rectified in subsequent printings if notice is given to the Publisher.

This book is dedicated to Steve Carter, who makes life better than I ever dreamed.

A big thank you to Margaret Smith of Kuretake UK Ltd for supplying the ZIG pens used in this book and to G.F. Smith & Son Ltd for their fabulous range of paper and card.

Many thanks also to all my friends at Search Press, especially Martin and Roz for giving me this opportunity, Sophie for her patience and Juan, Dave, Lotti and Inger for all their hard work and encouragement.

I would also like to say a special thank you to my family, my husband Steve and my friend Chantal for their support and advice.

The Publishers would like to say a huge thank you to Jessika Kwan, Ellie Hayward, Stephen Fay, Christopher Owens, Matthew Knight, Lucia Brisefer, Amy Weller, Lydia Rawley and Mahbub Ali.

Finally, special thanks to Southborough Primary School, Tunbridge Wells.

When this sign is used in the book, it means that adult supervision is needed.

REMEMBER!
Ask an adult to help you when you see this sign.

Contents

Introduction 4

Materials 6

Nazca Birds 8

Fantasy Planets 10

Matisse Collage 12

It's a Goal! 14

Spooky Wood 16

Funky Fish 18

Smiling Sunflower 20

Pop-up Dinosaur 22

Jazzy Guitar 24

Winter Window 26

Techniques 28

Patterns 29

Index 32

Introduction

Commercial greetings cards are sent for all sorts of reasons: to wish someone a happy birthday, or good luck; to celebrate a festival such as Christmas or New Year; to say thank you, congratulations, or just hello. A greetings card tells someone that you are thinking of them and that you care, and it gives them a picture to display in their home. Just think how much more special a handmade card is, because you have created it yourself and chosen the message personally.

People all over the world have been sending each other hand-decorated messages and cards for hundreds of years, probably since paper became widely available. The oldest known Valentine's card was made in the 1400s and is in the British Museum. Printed cards came later, in the nineteenth century, and were mainly for celebrating holidays or religious festivals.

In this book I show you how to make a variety of different cards using a range of materials including felt, pipe cleaners, beads and even wobbly plastic eyes! Do not worry if you think you cannot draw very well, as there are patterns in the back of the book to help you. I have also included a section on page 28 which shows you easy methods of transferring designs and scoring and folding card. There are lots of fun techniques to try like paint spattering, sewing and collage.

Inspiration can come from all sorts of sources. I usually think of the person I am making the card for, and that gets me started. In this book there are cards inspired by space, nature, musical instruments, dinosaurs, sport, famous artists and ancient wonders. Once you have chosen your subject, you can investigate it further by searching for information in libraries, galleries and museums and on the internet.

Nature is a very good place to find inspiration. You can collect leaves, sticks and flowers to make a collage, or look at the weather and the amazing effects it has on our world. Sometimes the materials themselves can be inspiring: just laying them out in front of you can be enough to trigger an idea and get you started.

Most importantly remember there are no rules; the more you experiment and dare to try something new, the more wonderful your cards will be. A card can be simple or complicated, take an hour to make or just five minutes. A greetings card is very special, it is a gift and a message all in one. Enjoy making them and people will enjoy receiving them.

Greetings cards first became really popular in Victorian times. This beautifully painted nineteenth century Christmas card shows the ornate and detailed style typical of the Victorians.

Materials

The items pictured here are the basic materials that you will need to make the projects in this book. Cards are not expensive to make and you can find a lot of the items shown here at home. Start collecting bits of coloured paper and card, pieces of string and ribbon, beads, buttons, pictures from magazines and even old greetings cards. You can cut these up and recycle them to create your own original designs. Soon you will have a box of treasures to dip into whenever you are feeling creative.

Coloured **pipe cleaners** are great fun and can be bent into almost any shape.

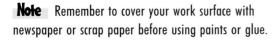

Note Remember to cover your work surface with newspaper or scrap paper before using paints or glue.

Pencils are used for drawing and to transfer designs. A **ballpoint pen** that has run out of ink is used to score card. **Compasses** are used to draw circles and to pierce holes.

A clear **sandwich bag** is used to create a window for the Winter Window card on page 26.

All sorts of **card** and **paper** can be used for making handmade cards. Coloured card is ideal and **corrugated** and **metallic card** can be very effective.

Coloured **pens** are used to draw and colour in designs. **Paint pens** and **metallic pens** are great because they show up on most coloured backgrounds. You can also use **felt-tipped pens**. A **thin black pen** is used to outline designs.

It is safest to use a **blunt-ended needle** like a tapestry needle for sewing.

Plastic eyes create lively characters and add movement to cards. **Beads** are used for decoration and **polystyrene balls** are excellent for creating snow.

Cutting your designs out of **high-density foam** gives them depth.

Pencil lines are rubbed out with an **eraser**. A **ruler** is used for measuring and to draw and score straight lines.

Fantastic paint effects can be created with an old **toothbrush** and a **sponge**.

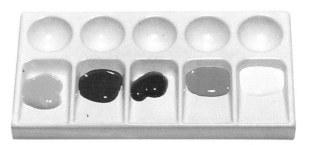

The **paints** used in this book are water-based. Acrylics, gouache or poster paints are best.

Clear **sticky tape** holds sandwich bags and thread in place. **Masking tape** is used to secure a design when transferring it.

Fabrics such as **felt** are great for adding texture. **Scissors** are used for cutting card, thread, fabric and high-density foam. Use an old pair for cutting sandpaper.

Place **thick corrugated cardboard** under your card when piercing holes. **Fine sandpaper** can be used to add texture.

Coloured and metallic **thread** is used for sewing and beading.

A **glue stick** is perfect for sticking paper and card. **Strong, clear glue** is used to stick on fabric and decorations.

Nazca Birds

In the 1930s, pilots were flying over the desert in Peru in South America when they saw giant drawings on the ground. There was a monkey the size of a football pitch, a lizard twice that length, a spider, fish, birds and insects. It is thought that they were made by the Nazca Indians around two thousand years ago, but nobody knows why. Have a look at them in a library or on the internet and try to imagine why they were made and how. This card is inspired by one of the Nazca drawings, of a large bird called a condor.

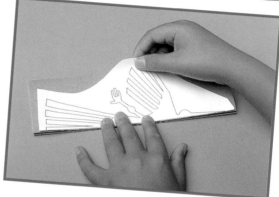

Ask an adult to help you to photocopy the design.

1 Fold a sheet of A4 fine sandpaper in half with the sand on the outside. Then fold the top layer in half again, back towards the centre fold. Turn the sandpaper over and fold the top layer in half as before so that you have four equal layers.

2 Photocopy the design on page 30. Cut round it roughly and stick it on to the folded sandpaper with a glue stick. Make sure that the dotted line that runs down one side of the pattern is up against the outer folds. Don't worry if the bird's wings overlap the edge.

3 Carefully cut out the bird shape. Make sure you do not cut off the ends of the feathers that have dotted lines. They should extend to meet the fold.

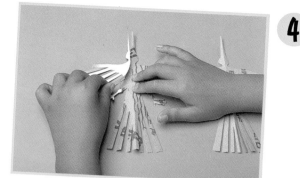

4 Open out the sandpaper to reveal two condors joined at the wings. Peel off the photocopied pattern. Do not worry if some parts will not peel off – they will not show.

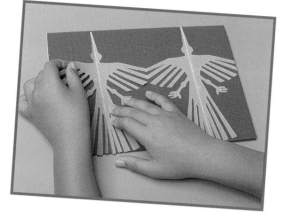

5 Score and fold a piece of A3 corrugated card in half widthways to make a card (see page 28).

6 Stick the condors on to the card with strong, clear glue.

FURTHER IDEAS

Invent your own fold-out Nazca style designs, using geometric shapes, straight lines and repeated patterns.

Fantasy Planets

Space ... the final frontier! What is out there? We know about the planets in our own solar system, but we cannot be sure about what lies beyond. Many people are fascinated by space and all the unanswered questions we have about the universe. With space, you can let your imagination run wild! In this project, spattering white paint on black card makes the perfect starry background for your own fantasy solar system. You can create all kinds of weird and wonderful planets using paint techniques and metallic pens.

YOU WILL NEED

Thick black card
Coloured card • Paints
Metallic pens • Pencil
Empty ballpoint pen • Ruler
Sponge • Toothbrush
Scissors • Compasses

1 Score and fold a large piece of black card in half. Dip the end of a toothbrush in some white paint and slowly run your finger over the bristles so the paint spatters onto the card. Allow to dry. You can spatter on a second colour if you like.

Note Practise spattering or sponging on scrap paper first, and always cover your work surface.

2 To make the planets, use compasses to draw four different sized circles on coloured card. Cut them out.

3 Put a circle on some newspaper. Dip a sponge in paint and lightly stroke the colour a little way across from one side. Stroking in a slight curve will make the planet look three-dimensional.

4

Sponge another colour across from the other side and then spatter more colours over the top with the toothbrush. Experiment with sponging, spattering and using metallic pens to decorate the other planets. Leave to dry.

5

Using the pattern on page 29 as a guide, draw a planet ring on card. Make sure it will fit over one of your planets. Then cut it out and lightly sponge some paint across it. Leave it to dry.

6

Slip the ring over a planet. Move the planets around on your space background until you are happy with the picture. Then stick them all in place with glue.

FURTHER IDEAS

Add aliens, rockets, meteors or space ships to your fantasy solar system.

Matisse Collage

Henri Matisse was a famous artist. He was influenced by many different styles. Once when Matisse was ill, he found it difficult to paint, so he made pictures by cutting shapes out of paper and sticking them down to make a collage. 'I am drawing directly in colour,' he said.

In this project I show you how to make a collage inspired by Matisse. There is a pattern on page 30 to help you, but if you feel confident, you could try cutting out your own picture freehand as Matisse did.

YOU WILL NEED

Thin card • Thick card
Compasses • Scissors
Empty ballpoint pen • Ruler
Glue stick • Pencil • Paper
Masking tape

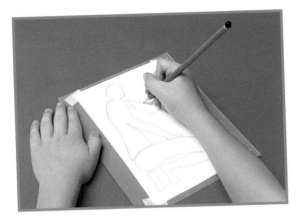

1 Transfer the pattern on page 30 on to thin card, or draw it freehand if you prefer.

2 On a different coloured piece of card, draw or transfer the plant design. Then, using compasses, draw a circle roughly 25mm (1in) across.

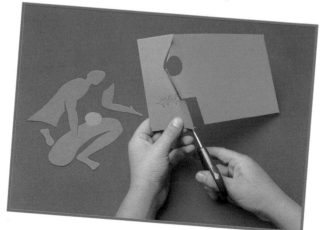

3 Cut out all of the shapes using scissors.

 4

Take an A5 piece of thin card and trim 5–10mm (¼in) off each side. Try to leave an uneven edge as you cut.

 5

Arrange the pieces on the card, leaving small gaps in the figure as shown. Glue them in place with a glue stick.

 6

Score and fold a piece of A4 card in half and stick the finished collage on to the front.

FURTHER IDEAS

Cut out the shapes for figures, animals or plants, to make your own original collages.

It's a Goal!

Soccer is a brilliant game to play and to watch. Its history dates as far back as the ancient Chinese, Greek, Mayan and Egyptian societies. Modern football developed from games played in England in the nineteenth century. In 1863 these games were separated into rugby football, which is where American football comes from, and Association football, or soccer. You can make this soccer goal card by sewing the net with coloured thread, attaching the goal posts and finally putting the ball in the net – one-nil!

 Score and fold a piece of thick A4 card in half. Stick a strip of green paper across the bottom.

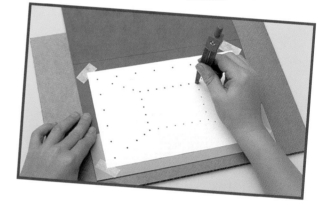

 Photocopy the dot pattern on page 31 and secure it to the front of the card with masking tape. Open the card and lay the front over a piece of thick corrugated cardboard to protect your work surface. Using the point of your compasses, pierce holes through the dots on the pattern. Then remove the pattern.

> (!) Ask an adult to help you to photocopy the design.

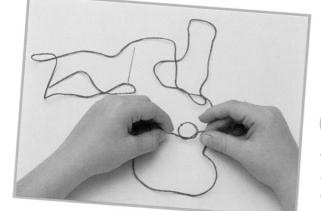

 Thread one end of a long piece of coloured thread through the eye of a blunt-ended needle. Tie a large knot in the other end.

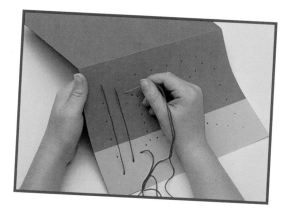

4

Push the needle up through the hole in the bottom left-hand corner and down through the hole in the top left-hand corner. Do the same for the next holes and continue until all the vertical lines are sewn.

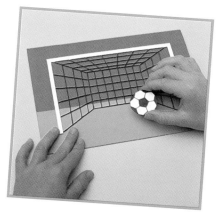

5

Now sew all the other lines of the net, as shown. You will use some holes more than once. If you run out of thread, tie a knot and thread your needle again.

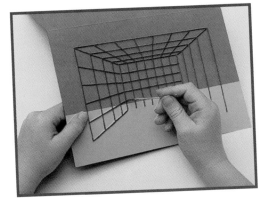

6

Transfer the goal posts and the football design on page 31 on to white card and cut them out. Colour the football with a black pen as shown. Use strong, clear glue to stick the goal posts and ball on to the card.

FURTHER IDEAS

Sew a basketball hoop, tennis racket, spider's web or even somebody's name to make an unusual card.

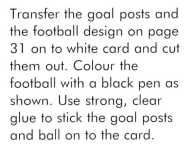

Spooky Wood

Woods can be very spooky at night. It is easy to imagine pairs of eyes peeping out from the dark. Woods and forests are often used to conjure up a spooky atmosphere in paintings, stories, poems and films. Collect interesting looking sticks and twigs to make the trees in this spooky wood card. Imagine the different creatures that live in the wood as you stick on their eyes. You could even write a spooky poem in the card.

YOU WILL NEED

Bright corrugated card • Thick card
Empty ballpoint pen • Ruler
Scissors • Plastic eyes
Masking tape • Pencil • Paper
Sticks • Strong, clear glue
Black felt

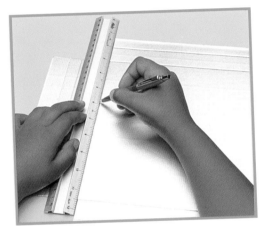

1 Enlarge the design on page 31 on a photocopier and transfer it on to the back of a piece of bright corrugated card. Enlarge the design by 141% to fit on to a sheet of A4, or by 200%, to fit on to a sheet of A3. Cut it out and score and fold along the dotted lines.

Ask an adult to help you to photocopy the design.

2 Fold up the left-hand side of the corrugated card to make a rectangular tube. Squeeze a line of strong, clear glue on to the corrugated side of the end tab and stick it in place. Do the same on the right, but leave the top and bottom open.

Measure the flat area left in the middle. Cut out a piece of black felt the same size. Stick it on with strong, clear glue.

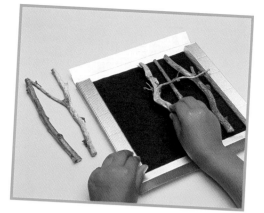

 4 Trim the sticks so they fit roughly inside the flat area. Then arrange them on top of the felt to look like a wood.

 **!**

Ask an adult to help you to cut the sticks.

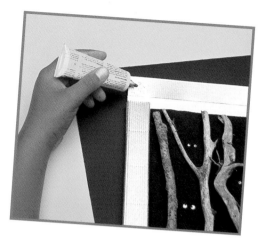

5 When you are happy with the picture, glue down the sticks with strong, clear glue. Then stick pairs of plastic eyes in between the sticks. Leave to dry.

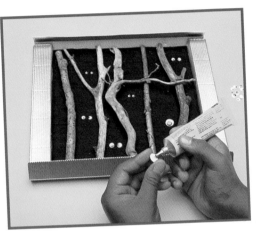

 6

Finish the frame by gluing the corners of the top and bottom flaps and sticking them down. Finally stick the finished frame on to a piece of folded card.

FURTHER IDEAS

Spray sticks with snow spray or silver paint and add a silvery moon to make a winter scene.

Funky Fish

Fish are very beautiful. It is amazing how many different shapes and colours there are. We have only explored one hundredth of the seabeds on our planet, so there may be even more weird and wonderful varieties of fish to be discovered in the future. In this project, fish are threaded on to metallic thread with beads, to make a bubbly underwater scene.

YOU WILL NEED

Thick card • Thin card
Coloured paper
Metallic thread • Compasses
Glue stick • Strong, clear glue
Sticky tape • Beads • Plastic eyes
Masking tape • Pencil
Empty ballpoint pen
Scissors

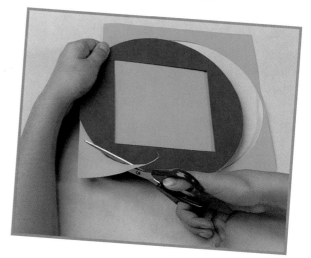

1 Score and fold a large piece of thick card in half. Using compasses and a pencil, draw a circle overlapping the fold and the bottom by about 5mm (¼in) as shown. Cut it out.

2 Open the circular card and draw a square on the front. Cut out the square to make a window. Stick a piece of coloured paper on the inside back of the card (the side you can see through the window) and trim to size.

Fold three small pieces of thin coloured card in half. Transfer one of the fish designs on page 29 on to each piece of card. Cut out the fish – you will end up with two of each design.

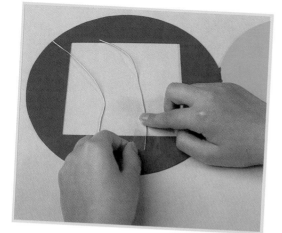

4

Lay two pieces of metallic thread over the window on the inside of the card. Secure them at the bottom with sticky tape.

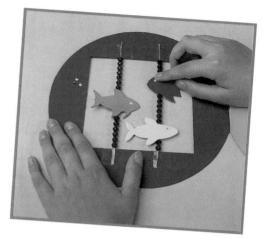

5

Thread some beads on to the first piece of metallic thread. Then take a pair of fish and put glue on one of them. Stick the fish together, sandwiching the thread between them as shown.

6

Thread on more beads and secure the top of the thread with sticky tape. Do the same on the other thread, using more beads and the other two fish. Finally stick plastic eyes on both sides of the fish using strong, clear glue.

FURTHER IDEAS

Make a card with a different shaped window. Add other sea creatures — an octopus, seahorse or dolphin.

Smiling Sunflower

Flowers are often used to cheer people up, and for special occasions like Mother's day and Valentine's day. Different flowers can mean different things. Red flowers are usually for love – roses, carnations and tulips. White flowers such as daisies and lilies represent innocence and purity. Pansies and poppies are for remembrance, sweet peas for goodbyes, and forget-me-nots speak for themselves! Sunflowers turn their heads to follow the sun across the sky. This one has a lovely smile and a stem made from flexible pipe cleaners, so that its head bobs cheerfully when it moves.

YOU WILL NEED

Card • Pipe cleaners
Scissors • Ruler • Pen
Plastic eyes • Pencil
Masking tape • Paper
Compasses • Eraser • Felt
Empty ballpoint pen
Strong, clear glue

2 Cut a slit from the edge up to the small circle. Then cut a second slit next to it. Continue all of the way around the face. Carefully erase the pencil circle.

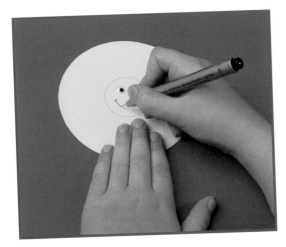

3 Fold every other petal away from you until there is a space between each one. Then hold all the folded petals together and wrap the end of a pipe cleaner round them until they are secure. The rest of this pipe cleaner will be the sunflower's stem.

1 Use compasses and a pencil to draw a large circle on some yellow card, then cut it out. Draw a smaller circle in the middle for the sunflower's face. Stick on plastic eyes using strong, clear glue, and draw on a smile.

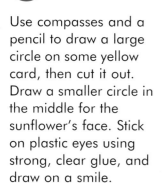

Twist more pipe cleaners around the stem to make it longer and thicker. Cut two sets of leaves out of felt. Push the leaves between the pipe cleaners as shown.

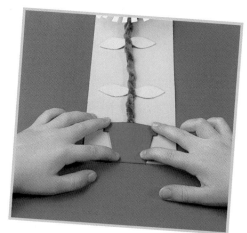

5

Transfer the pattern for the flower pot on page 29 on to card. Cut it out. Score along the dotted lines as shown and fold back the tabs.

6

Score and fold a piece of A4 size card in half lengthways. Glue the bottom half of the flower stem to the card. Put glue on the flower pot tabs and stick the pot over the stem.

FURTHER IDEAS
Create flowers using textured papers or metallic card. Try making several layers of petals.

Pop-up Dinosaur

Millions of years ago there were no people, and dinosaurs ruled the earth. We know from digging up their bones what kinds of dinosaurs existed, their sizes and shapes and even what they ate. But we do not know what colours they were. So when you make this pop-up dinosaur card, imagine the colours for yourself and create a prehistoric world of your own. There are patterns for the Tyrannosaurus Rex and the Pteranodon in the back of the book, but you could draw any of your favourite dinosaurs – or even invent your own.

YOU WILL NEED

Thick card • Scissors
Coloured and metallic paint pens
Strong, clear glue • Pencil
Ruler • Masking tape • Paper
Thin black pen • Acrylic paint
Natural sponge

Score and fold a large piece of thick card in half. On the top half of the inside, sponge on a strip of paint to suggest a landscape. Leave to dry.

Note Sponging two similar colours on top of each other can make a landscape look more realistic.

2 Transfer the Tyrannosaurus Rex and Pteranodon designs on page 30 on to thick card. Colour them in using paint pens.

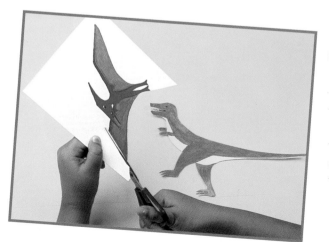

3 Draw the outlines and the eyes with a thin black pen. Carefully cut the dinosaurs out. If some areas are difficult to cut out, colour them black so that they will not show up.

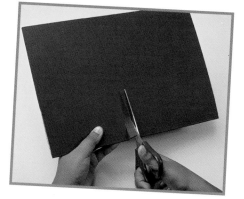

Decide where you want your dinosaur to stand, and mark the spot lightly with a pencil. Fold the card inside out. From the fold side, cut two slits up to the mark you have made.

5

Open up the card and press between the cuts to push out a tab. Then close the card again with the tab pushed out and press. This will help to fold the tab in the right position.

6

Open the card and stick the Tyrannosaurus's leg on to the tab with strong, clear glue. Glue the Pteranodon on to the background.

Note To make the Pteranodon stand out from the card, stick a little pad of folded card on the back before gluing it in place.

FURTHER IDEAS
Make pop-up scenery for your dinosaur world: hills, trees, plants, mountains — even a volcano!

Jazzy Guitar

Guitars are played all over the world to make all kinds of music – from Spanish flamenco and folk music to pop, rock and jazz. They usually have six strings, although there are twelve-string guitars as well. The strings play a different note depending on how taut they are. They can be adjusted to the right pitch using a special tuning key. You can make a card in the shape of a guitar and add strings made from coloured thread.

YOU WILL NEED

Card • Scissors
Glue stick • Pencil • Paper
Masking tape • Compasses
Coloured thread • Blunt-ended needle
Thick corrugated cardboard
Paint pens

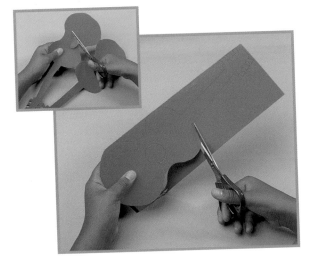

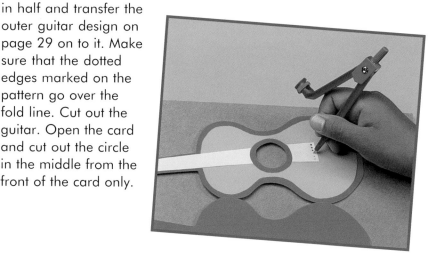

1 Score and fold a piece of thick coloured card in half and transfer the outer guitar design on page 29 on to it. Make sure that the dotted edges marked on the pattern go over the fold line. Cut out the guitar. Open the card and cut out the circle in the middle from the front of the card only.

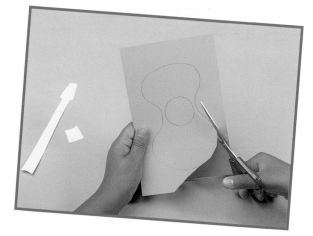

2 Transfer the inner guitar pattern and the neck and soundboard patterns on to coloured card and cut them out.

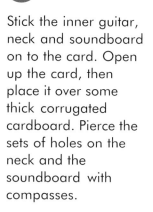

3 Stick the inner guitar, neck and soundboard on to the card. Open up the card, then place it over some thick corrugated cardboard. Pierce the sets of holes on the neck and the soundboard with compasses.

 Thread one end of a piece of coloured thread through the eye of a blunt-ended needle and tie a knot in the other end. Sew up through the far left hole at the bottom and down through the far left hole at the top.

Gently pull the thread through until taut. Do not pull it too tight, or the card will bend. Then wrap the end round the bottom left tuning key and tie a knot. Repeat for the other five strings.

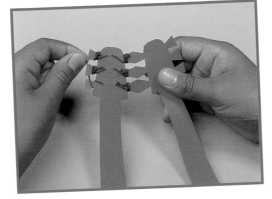

 Decorate your guitar by drawing big dots around the edge with a paint pen.

Note If you find knotting the thread difficult, you can tape the loose ends at the back.

FURTHER IDEAS

Try making other musical instruments. A banjo has five strings, a double bass has four and a harp has lots and lots.

Winter Window

Many cultures around the world have a winter festival. Most of them are linked to the winter solstice. This is the time of the shortest day and the longest night of the year. Some of the festivals celebrated during winter are Christmas, Bodhi Day, Hanukkah and Yule. Winter is a lovely time to gather with family and friends and stay warm by the fire. You can make a winter window card using polystyrene balls for snow and a clear plastic bag such as a sandwich or freezer bag for the window.

1

Cut out two pieces of card, one 42cm x 21cm (16½in x 8¼in), and one 21cm (8¼in) square. Fold the big one in half.

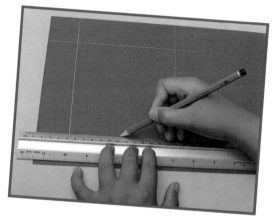

2 On the inside front of the folded card, measure 4cm (1½in) in from each side and draw lines to make a square. Cut out the square.

3

Open up the card again and lay a clear sandwich bag over the square. You may need to trim the top of the bag to fit. Use sticky tape to stick it on at the bottom and sides. Do not stretch the bag too tightly, as this will warp the card.

4

Draw a tree on high-density foam and cut it out. Put a line of glue down the middle of the tree and stick it inside the bag. Make sure the glued side of the tree is uppermost.

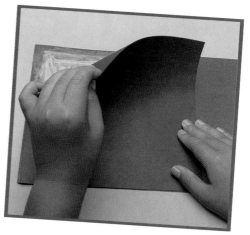

5

Sprinkle some polystyrene balls in to the bag and tape up the top.

6

Spread strong, clear glue on the inside of the card window frame. Stick the square piece of card on top.

FURTHER IDEAS

You can make all sorts of things to stand in your snow storm – try a snowman, a house, a reindeer or a penguin.

Techniques

Ask an adult to help you to photocopy the patterns.

Transferring a design

You can photocopy the patterns on pages 29–31 and transfer them on to card using the technique shown below. Use the photocopier to enlarge or reduce the designs if you need to.

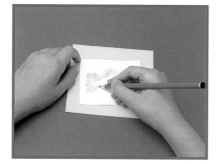  

1 Photocopy the design. Turn over the photocopy and scribble over the lines with a soft pencil.

2 Turn the photocopy over and tape it to your card using masking tape. Then go over the lines of the design with a pencil.

3 Peel back the photocopy to reveal the transferred design.

Scoring and folding card

Dotted lines on the patterns need to be scored and folded. You can also use scoring to help make neat cards. Find the centre line by measuring the halfway point and score and fold as shown below.

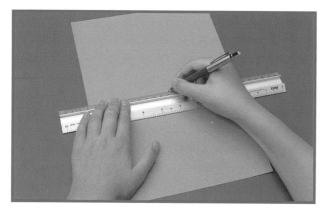 

1 Score a line across the middle of the card with a ballpoint pen that has run out of ink.

2 Fold the card and run the back of your fingernail along the fold to press it down. If the edges are not exactly square, you can trim them with scissors.

Patterns

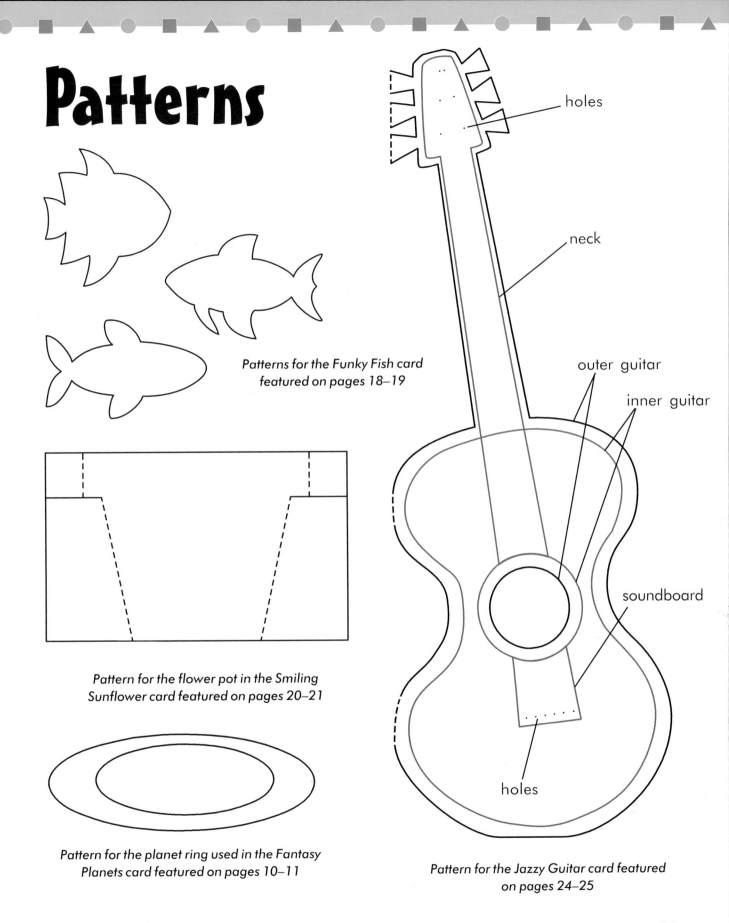

Patterns for the Funky Fish card
featured on pages 18–19

Pattern for the flower pot in the Smiling
Sunflower card featured on pages 20–21

Pattern for the planet ring used in the Fantasy
Planets card featured on pages 10–11

holes

neck

outer guitar

inner guitar

soundboard

holes

Pattern for the Jazzy Guitar card featured
on pages 24–25

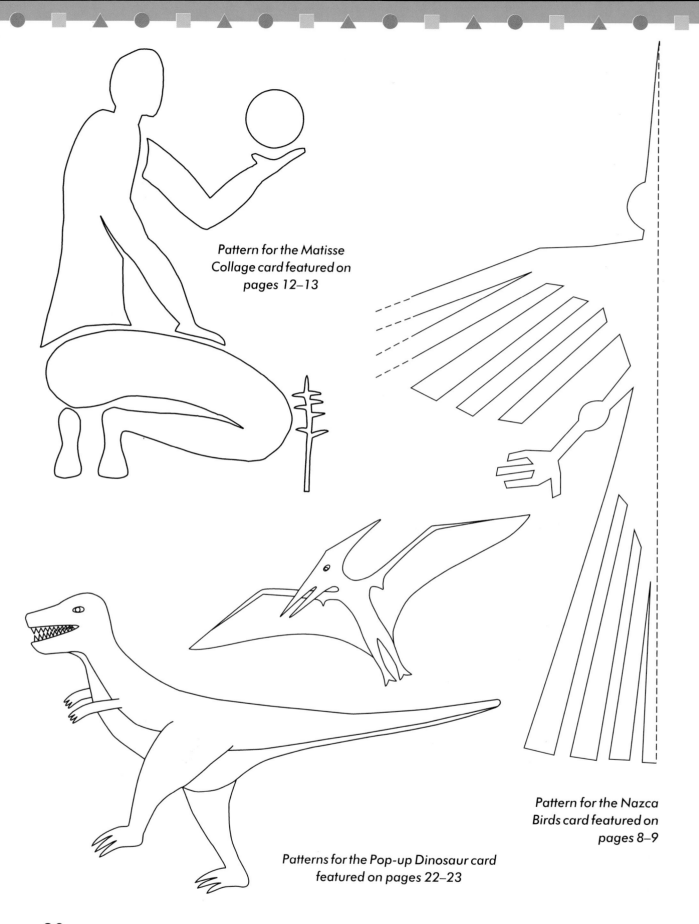

Pattern for the Matisse Collage card featured on pages 12–13

Pattern for the Nazca Birds card featured on pages 8–9

Patterns for the Pop-up Dinosaur card featured on pages 22–23

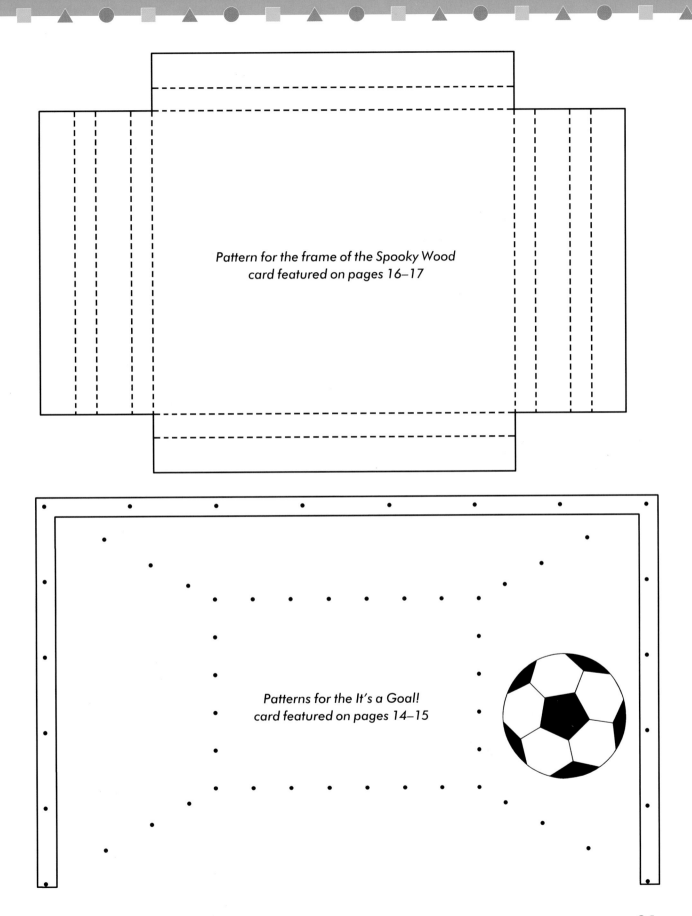

Pattern for the frame of the Spooky Wood
card featured on pages 16–17

Patterns for the It's a Goal!
card featured on pages 14–15

Index

artists 4, 12

beads 4, 7, 18, 19

collage 4, 12, 13, 30

compasses 6, 10, 12, 14, 18, 20, 24

dinosaurs 4, 22, 23, 31

fabric 7

felt 4, 7, 16, 17, 20, 21

festivals 4, 26

flowers 4, 20, 21, 29

folding 4, 8, 9, 10, 13, 14, 16, 18, 21, 22, 23, 26, 28

football 14, 15

frame 17, 30

glue 7, 8, 9, 11, 12, 13, 14, 15, 16, 17, 18, 19, 20, 21, 23, 24, 26, 27

high-density foam 7, 26, 27

Matisse 12–13, 30

metallic pens 6, 10, 11

Mother's day 20

Nazca Indians 8–9, 30

needle 7, 14, 15, 24, 25

paint 7, 10, 12, 17, 22

paint pens 6, 22, 24, 25

paper 4, 6, 7, 8, 12, 14, 16, 17, 20, 21, 22, 23, 26

photocopy 8, 9, 14, 16, 28

pipe cleaners 4, 6, 20, 21

planets 10, 11, 18, 29

plastic eyes 4, 7, 16, 17, 18, 19, 20

polystyrene balls 7, 26, 27

Pteranodon 22–23

sandpaper 7, 8, 9

sandwich bag 6, 7, 26–27

scoring 4, 9, 10, 13, 14, 16, 18, 21, 22, 24, 28

sewing 4, 7, 14, 15, 25

space 4, 10, 11

spattering 4, 10, 11

sponge 7, 10, 11, 22

sticks 4, 16, 17

sticky tape 7, 18, 19, 26

sunflowers 20–21, 29

thread 7, 14, 15, 18, 19, 24, 25

toothbrush 7, 10, 11

transferring design 6, 12, 18, 21, 22, 24, 27, 28

Tyrannosaurus Rex 22–23

Valentine's day 4, 20

Victorian 5

window 6, 18, 19, 26–27